I SURF, THEREFORE I AM

Works by Peter Kreeft from St. Augustine's Press

The Sea Within: Waves and the Meaning of All Things

If Einstein Had Been a Surfer

Socratic Logic: A Logic Text Using Socratic Method, Platonic Questions, and Aristotelian Principles

Summa Philosophica

The Philosophy of Jesus

Jesus-Shock

I SURF, THEREFORE I AM
A Philosophy of Surfing

PETER KREEFT

ST. AUGUSTINE'S PRESS
South Bend, Indiana
2008

Manufactured in the United States of America.

2 3 4 5 6   17 16 15 14 13 12 11

Library of Congress Cataloging in Publication Data

Kreeft, Peter.
I surf, therefore I am: a philosophy of surfing /
Peter Kreeft.
p. cm.
ISBN-13: 978-1-58731-377-6 (hardbound: alk. paper)
ISBN-10: 1-58731-377-4 (hardbound: alk. paper)
1. Surfing. I. Title.
GV839.5.K74 2008
797.3'2 – dc22   2007040597

∞ *The paper used in this publication meets the minimum
requirements of the American National Standard for
Information Sciences – Permanence of Paper for Printed
Materials, ANSI Z39.48-1984.*

St. Augustine's Press
www.staugustine.net

Contents

Non-Introduction

This book is for three kinds of people:

1. for curious non-surfers, it is a confession;
2. for surfers, it is a manifesto; and
3. for wannabe surfers, it is a practical beginners' handbook.

Why should you read this book?

Because surfing makes you so ridiculously happy that it makes you happy just to read about it, and it makes me happy just to write about it.

If that's not a good enough reason, go enjoy your misery.

Good introductions should be short.

Ten Reasons Why Everyone Should Surf

There are ten reasons why everybody should surf. Ten great sages teach these ten reasons. In this book we will surf on the sages, and then we will surf on the sea.

Reason #1: Because It Makes You Happy (Aristotle)
(Why Surfers Smile)

Aristotle raises the most important question in the world, in his *Ethics*: what is the point, purpose, end, good, or goal of everything in human life? In other words, what is the greatest good? And he gives the obviously right answer: happiness. Everybody does everything that they do for that reason, nobody does anything for any other reason, and nobody pursues happiness for any other reason than itself. No one says, "What good is happiness? It can't buy money." But some people say, "What good is money? It can't buy happiness." (And other people disagree with that.)

Philosophers like Aristotle, scientists like Freud, and ordinary people like yourself all agree that happiness is the natural end of everything we do.

So the very best reason to surf is to make you happy.

Does it work?

Let's ask.

"Why do you surf?" is a legitimate question. Surfing costs something. Not in money (a hundred dollars for a board makes it one of the cheapest thrills in this world), but in time, which is more important than money because money is not life but time is life. (We call it our "life-time"). To surf, especially in our era of "have no time – too busy,"[1] you have to *not*-do a thousand other things, like compare ten different insurance policies, or clean toilet bowls, or watch chattering meatheads on TV that make "heydude" surfers look like rocket scientists.

We're messed up because we did not listen to Aristotle, who said that there are only three reasons why anybody ever should do anything: because it's morally good, because it's practically necessary, or because it delights you.

---

1 This is our definition of "progress": each generation having less time (and therefore less life) than the previous one. Why? Because of all our time-saving devices, i.e. our technology. Surfing frees you from the worship of technology. (The problem is not the machines but the mind-set, of course.)

Aristotle also said that work is for leisure, not leisure for work.

We have not "progressed" if we have forgotten these elementary truths.

There are risks to surfing. Change just one letter and "surfer" becomes "suffer." Surfers have scars. (Actually very few surfers, on all levels, have ever been injured enough to need medical attention. It's about the same proportion of New Yorkers who have been mugged. It's closer to one in a hundred than to one in ten.) But they laugh at the scrapes and go back for more. Why?

Here are 25 typical answers to the question "Why do you surf?" that I've collected over the years. They're some first-hand testimony of what surfing does to you.

(1) "To get that silly smile on your face."

(2) "To escape. To be free from the land, with all its ropes and chains and walls."

(3) "Not to be wiped out but to be wiped. The sea wipes away your tears with one great big wipe. It wipes your bum too. It's Mommy."

(4) "To be what we are: sea creatures. Seals and dolphins surf too."

(5) "To be an astronaut. To escape earth's orbit."

(6) "It's like falling in love. It just happens."

(7) "To go to Heaven and see God."

(8) "Because one good wave makes your whole miserable day worthwhile."

(9) "To get into something that's straight out of your dreams."

(10) "Just to be there with Her. Even when there's no surf, She's still there."

(11) "To play. To be little. To turn time back."

(12) "To be drunk and sober at the same time."

(13) "Because it gives you energy instead of taking it. You have more inner energy after it than before."

(14) "Because it's a Total Stress Eraser. You come out washed in body, soul, and spirit."

(15) "Because when you're in the trough of a wave, you're in the lap of God. Nothing can touch you."

(16) "Because nothing else puts you inside the biggest and most beautiful thing you will ever see in this world."

(17) "Because surfers are happy. The whole world envies surfers, because the world wants you to be happy only in ways it can understand and control."

(18) "Because you learn who you are with each

wipeout: a happy fool. It teaches you humility, and wisdom, and the need to suffer a little to be happy a lot."

(19) "Because, you see, the sea is a little bit like God."

(20) "Because surfing goes beyond the either-or of giving or taking. You can't take anything away from the ocean except the joy that keeps multiplying and can't be divided. And you can't give the ocean anything except your joy, to be multiplied some more."

(21) "Because that's all there is. Everything is some form of surfing. You surf on breath, and food, and money, and work, and sex, and religion. Whatever it is, you paddle out to it, you pull into it, you ride it, you pull out of it. Surfing on the ocean is just the biggest and best kind of surfing."

(22) "Because it's the answer to life's greatest mystery. It gives you what every human being is after here on earth. And what's that? I just told you: it's life's greatest mystery. If I told you more, it wouldn't be."

(23) "Because even the most perfect words are inadequate to answer that question, and even the most imperfect surfing is more than adequate to answer that question."

(24) "Because waves are free psychiatrists."

(25) "Just do it and you'll see why."

A survey asked ten young surfers the question their mothers must have asked them: What do you want to do with your life, just surf till you die? The answers were:

(a) Sure,

(b) Yup,

(c) Yep,

(d) You betcha,

(e) Sure hope so,

(f) Right,

(g) Damnright,

(h) Why not?

(i) Yeah, and

(j) (from a surfer in Maine) Ayup

Obviously, surfers are happy.

Are they fanatics? I feel creepy around fanatics.

No, surfers are not fanatics, because fanatics are not happy and surfers are.

Nobody *seems* more fanatical than surfers. Golfers come close, but they are not as loyal to their "thing" as surfers are. Half the golfers in the world, at one time or another in their golf lives, have cursed their game, and even smashed their clubs, and vowed to give up the habit, like smokers. But not a surfer in the world has ever cursed surfing or smashed his board or vowed to give it up. Never. Not even after the gnarliest wipeouts, near drownings, broken bones, deafness, paralysis, shark attacks, or even severed limbs. One paralyzed surfer even surfs in his wheelchair, which is attached to his board.

A survey once asked a cross-section of 200 surfers two questions: (1) Would you give up surfing for a million dollars? (2) Would you give up surfing if you knew you were getting surfer's ear? (Surfer's ear is quite common in winter surfers It comes from repeated exposure to cold water, which makes the bones around the ear canal grow to protect the eardrum, thus eventually blocking the ear canal and making you deaf. Operations to cure it are very painful and usually need to be repeated.) The answers varied from "get real" and "get a life" to "get out of my house."

How many golfers would give up golf for a million dollars? Some of them try to give it up for nothing.

Surfers are not aliens, weirdos, terrorists, or fundamentalists. (Not many fundamentalists are surfers. The two contradict each other.

Fundamentalists believe the Rapture is future; surfers know it's present.) I know of two city mayors, seven published authors, two tycoons, one Hollywood director, and dozens of professional baseball, football, basketball, and hockey players who surf, as well as hundreds of doctors, lawyers, nurses, schoolteachers, university professors, and artists.

Everyone is a wannabe surfer. Watch at any beach. Most swimmers try to ride the waves. Few succeed. Yet they never give up trying.

No surfer in human history has ever uttered the following sentence: "That's enough waves. I'm bored." We could surf all day, every day, forever. Unlike almost everything else in life, surfing has no inner limits. All its limits are *outside* it, in the hard, cruel world with edges; not *inside* it. For waves have no edges.

On any given day when the sea is anything but hopelessly flat, in any given weather, however wet or windy or raw, you can see surfers bobbing on the swells like rubber duckies. You see them not only in sunny California but in freezing Hampton Beach, New Hampshire, and Nantasket Beach, Massachusetts, and Newport and Narragansett, Rhode Island, and Ditch Plains in Montauk, Long

Island, and Manasquan Inlet, New Jersey, just looking for a wave, longing for a wave, praying for just one good wave that will "make my day." You see these lean and hungry love-slaves sitting on their boards for hours waiting for just one rideable wave. If nature and nature's God does not will to make one today, these religious devotees will come back tomorrow hoping for the miracle. They will ride one-foot slop if they can find nothing better. They are like lapdog spaniels panting pathetically, tails wagging wildly, desperately hoping for just one tiny note of recognition from their mysterious mistress with the salty mouth.

I once saw a group of male surfers staring out to sea so hypnotized by a set of grade-A waves that they didn't even notice two grade-A girls in bikinis walking past. One girl looked annoyed at their inattention, the other smiled knowingly. Guess which girl knew a surfer.

Where else do you find such fidelity in the world today? Do you find golfers out on midwinter ice, on frozen turf? Do you find tennis players playing on hillsides if there are no flat courts? Baseball players don't even play in the rain!

Surfers are dazed because they're in love. The object of their love, the sea, is reflected in their faces. They always have that faraway look that comes from standing at a surf break gazing out to sea checking out the waves, waiting, waiting. Surfers spend more time waiting for waves than riding them. This gives them great patience. This is one reason no war in history has ever been started by surfers. If surfers ruled the world, there would be universal peace.

Watch their faces as closely as they watch the face of the water, and you will see what they are watching for, waiting for: you will see the traces of seawater in the gleam in their eyes and the shape of waves in the curve of their glance. Indoors, they always gravitate toward windows. That's how you can tell surfers at parties.

They keep doing this even in death. Ron Drummond, the author of the world's first surfing manual, *The Art of Wave Riding,* in 1931 (I have a copy! Precious!), wrote:

> *Bury me close to the clear green sea*
> *Where the crashing waves will spray over me,*
> *Where my soul will rise with the rising sun*
> *And be surfing still when the day is done. . . .*
> *It matters not where my grave will be,*
> *As long as it lies by a surging sea.*

Yes, I know most great sea poetry has been about ships and sailing, not about beaches and surfing. But that does not prove surfing is less poetic. (1) For one thing, the great English writers knew nothing about surfing until the 20th century. (2) For another thing, sailing gets less poetic the closer you get to it, while surfing gets *more*. Sailors don't find life aboard ship nearly as poetic as land-lubbers do. But surfers find surfing even more poetic than non-surfers do. (3) To surfers, ships are just overgrown, overcrowded surfboards. (4) Finally, surfing is *playing* with the sea, for sheer pleasure, while shipping is *working* with the sea, for profit. So which is more poetic?

The sea herself is the most poetic thing on earth (except perhaps a woman's face), and a break-ing wave is the most poetic thing on the sea, and riding it is the most poetic thing you can do with it. Therefore surfing is the most poetic thing you can do on earth. (See? Surfaholics are *logical*.)[2]

Fanatics are not poetic. Surfers are. Therefore surfers are not fanatics.

You can prove surfers are not fanatics by their

2 The author has written a popular and practical do-it-your-self textbook on logic, *Socratic Logic* (South Bend, Ind.: St. Augustine's Press, 2005), so he knows what "logical" means.

noses. Fanatics always have their "nose to the grind-stone." But surfers' noses are up in the heavens.

The next chapter explores those heavens, and proves that surfing is in a real and literal sense a mystical experience.

Reason #2: Because It Makes You Mystical (Buddha)
(Stoke as Nirvana)

No, my title is not meant to be an exaggeration. Surfing can easily be a truly mystical experience, far, far out beyond the most distant sandbars of language. It is ineffable. (So in writing about this, I am trying to eff the ineffable, or unscrew the inscrutable.)

Surfers have a word for this unique experience: "stoke." What other human activity has a unique word for the unique "high" it gives? Only two: "orgasm" and "Nirvana."

"Stoke" doesn't mean just "a high" but the unique, peculiar high that nothing but surfing can give. To say that the joy of surfing is simply one joy among many others is like saying that the earth is merely one planet among others, or that for Dante Beatrice is just one woman among others. (Say that to Dante and he will challenge you to a duel!) Stoke is no more interchangeable with any other joys, to a surfer, than Beatrice is interchangeable with any other women, to Dante.

In fact, surfing is very much like falling in love. You don't just fall in love with "women" or "men." You fall in love with Juliet, or Romeo. What you see with the newly opened "third eye" of love is the absolute uniqueness of the beloved. Similarly, surfing is unique because stoke is unique – as unique as the sea herself.

Like love, stoke is both indefinable and irresistible. Your first wave will hook you forever, like a fish. Listen to the classic account of how it happened to Jack London in Hawaii:

> One after another they came, a mile long, with smoking crests . . . these bull-mouthed monsters, and they weigh a thousand tons, and they charge into shore faster than a man can run. . . . I watched the little Kanaka boys. When a likely-looking breaker came along, they flopped upon their stomachs on their boards, kicked like mad with their feet, and rode the breaker into the beach. I tried to emulate them. I watched them, tried to do everything that they did, and failed utterly. The breaker swept past and I was not on it . . .

away the little rascals would scoot while I remained in disgust behind. I tried for a solid hour, and not one wave could I persuade to boost me shoreward.

Then, finally, at the end of the day, Jack caught his first wave, and (in his own words)

. . . from that moment I was lost.

Every surfer in the world can identify with that sentence.

Everyone remembers when he caught his first good wave.

And everyone remembers how he caught it. It wasn't by calculation or technology or book knowledge or logic but by instinct. It was like dancing. When you dance, you just *fall into the music*. You forget yourself. Well, in surfing, the wave is the music.

What does it feel like? When you catch your first good wave, you will feel gratitude, because you will know that you have not chosen it, it has chosen you. You have simply put yourself into the holy place where the gift was given.

You will feel *tiny*. You will feel as if you are being gripped and lifted up like a baby tiger in its mother's jaws, or swept up onto the cowcatcher on a steam locomotive. You will feel you are riding a foamy torpedo that has been shot to shore. You will feel wild abandon, like the nuclear cowboy riding the bomb in the last scene of *Dr. Strangelove*. You will want to *whoop*. Not many things in life make you want to whoop.

You will feel awe because you are riding one of the horses of the gods. Of all the metaphors for waves, perhaps the best is *stallions*. When the off-shore wind whips the crest of the approaching swells and leaves a halo of white spray behind each wave just before it plunges over, and if they are backlit by the sun, you will not be able *not* to see the waves as heavenly horses with wild white manes, ghost riders from the sky who disappear as quickly as they come.

And that fact can give you another feeling: pity. For that wave let you ride him at the last moment of his life, and his life was consummated for you. He died so that something in you could come to life in his death. (Waves are like Jesus that way.) You may also feel a sudden sadness when you reflect that only a very few of the millions of waves that have offered themselves to us on every beach in the world for millions of years have ever been consummated and ridden by surfers.

Most of all, you will feel hopelessly in love. From the moment of your first wave, you are doomed. Lost forever. Once you go to Heaven, you don't come back to earth.

* * * * *

Stoke is mystical because it transcends time.

It makes time reverse itself – not in the outer world physically, but inside you, mentally. There, it's a real time machine. It actually does to time what the poet can only long for:

Backward, turn backward,
O time in thy flight.
Make me a child again
Just for one night.

Surfing really does that, and not just for one night. Eighty-year-old surfers say it's just as thrilling after 70 years of surfing as it was on their first wave. Watch these old fogies becoming children again. You can literally see the magic in their eyes. Watch the pure, childlike joy arise on their faces like a swell on the sea, when that great cosmic force, wearing a wave as its clothing, overtakes them and lifts them up into Heaven, into eternity, out of time, out of sight of land. Your spirit can "catch the wave" of stoke on their face as their board catches the wave of water on the sea.

There's a second way surfing transcends time. Not only does it make time turn back, it makes time stop entirely. It makes time stand still for that one timeless moment when you and the wave are one, there at the top, as you catch it exactly at the split second when it breaks.

How big is that "split second" or "timeless moment"? So big that it contains the entire history of the universe, from the Big Bang right up to and including the act of drawing in your breath one instant before that wave-catching moment, that end of time, that apocalypse.

How paradoxical! – it's a *wave,* after all, utterly temporal and always moving, that is the vehicle of timelessness. The experience is pure paradox: it is the experience of the most dynamic, dynamite-like movement and the most standstill shock at once. For it's an experience of eternity, and eternity is not static but dynamic, like God.

Maybe that's why it makes us happy: because we weren't meant to be in time forever, but in timelessness forever. Maybe surfing brings us back to the timelessness of Eden. Maybe Adam and Eve felt that way all the time: exactly the way a surfer feels atop a wave.

Stephen Wright, the dour Boston comedian, says: "You know that feeling you get when you lean back in your chair and lift your feet up and balance on the two back legs of the chair for just one moment before you fall either forward or backward? Well, that's how I feel all the time." He's not at home in this solid world; he must be a surfer.

Maybe Adam and Eve in the Garden of Eden surfed the land as surfers surf the sea. Maybe their very earth was experienced as sea, as undulating, floating islands – like C.S. Lewis's *Perelandra*.

Stoke is happiness, but it's a mystical happiness. It's the kind that never bores you. It's *joy*. It surprises you every time, like a sudden kiss. Stoke is happiness, but it's the kind that isn't fleeting. It's like a lightning bolt that does not go away but stands there shining.

Other things make you happy before it but not after it (like forbidden pleasures that are destructive), or else after it but not before it (like doing your duty and obeying your conscience and being courageous); but surfing makes you happy before, during, and after. If I surf in the afternoon, that makes me happy all morning and evening too. A day of surfing is like a wave, with a long, grand swell *before* it breaks and a glorious spash *when* it breaks and a great whitewaterwash *after* it breaks.

Before: As you anticipate it for the thousandth time it's like the first time, like first love. Before you even hit the water you get Anticipation Stoke: you walk (or run) across the beach with a spring in your step and a song in your heart. And then you throw yourself into the miraculously healing waters like the cripple at the pool of Siloam, when you see the angel troubling the water with waves. (That's some powerful angel!)

During: Time stops when you catch the wave. The wave is like the lightning bolt. To catch it, you have to meet the timeless moment. If time doesn't stop for you, you don't catch it. If you stay in time and wait half a second longer, the wave is past; and if you run ahead too fast and enter the wave's time stream half a second too early, you get creamed. It is literally a split second, like a split coconut, and into that split you can fit eternity.

It's like that magic moment in *Our Town* when the dead Emily sees her life-in-time with the eyes of eternity.

Or like that magic moment in *The Miracle*

Worker when Helen Keller wakes to the meaning of meaning when Annie Sullivan spells out "water" into her hand down by the well.

Or like that one last miraculous moment experienced by the lonely, abused, and dying sister on the white swing in the yellow sun and the green grass in Ingmar Bergman's *Cries and Whispers* when her voice-over mind says that everything is good because this moment is the *only* moment. There is no other moment. This moment is the meaning of all moments. Perfection.

After: You're still stoked, with Post-Stoke Stoke. The sea somehow keeps loving you, washing over you and sweeping through your soul, even after your body comes out of it – like a mother loving her baby after the baby comes out of her womb. Mother Sea's rhythms and music are inscribed in your memory, and in your blood, and in your very genes, like the wave's prints on the sand. Your body rocks all night as you keep feeling the waves of the waves.

So surfing is a trinity of stoke: I will surf, I surf, I surfed.

That's not clever wordplay. It's unclever realplay. It happens. It works. It does things to you. It cleans out your soul. It's the answer to drugs.

Why does anyone do drugs? For the high. Drugs are fake mysticism. We are programmed to be mystics, and if we have neither the experience of the real thing nor the hope of it, we have to sell our souls to fake versions of it.

But stoke is a better high than drugs. You get higher on a wave than on a weed. And there are no bad side-effects, only good ones. No scrambled brains, no scrambled lives. And it's free. And it's good for your soul because it makes you happy and patient and nice. But not dull and uncreative and conformist. And it's good for your body because it's healthy outdoor exercise. I can tell the President how to win the war against drugs: get all the druggies to surf. That will lower the crime rate by half. America's streets won't be safe until we have a surfer President.

Surfing makes all your senses come alive more intensely than acid does, because it plunges you into truth and reality, not hallucination. Surfing makes you turn outward, not inward. It's just the opposite of hallucination. The feel of the hot caressing sun and the cold slap of the wave, and the taste and smell of brine, and the sound of the booming and roaring, and the sight of that falling blue mountain with a gaping maw ready to devour your electrically trembling body and suck you out of it and into ecstasy – this is a total sensory immersion in that greatest of all works of art that we call the universe.

When pressed to be more specific about the thrill in stoke, everyone mentions the *power*. Not yours – the sea's. This is the one thing that always absolutely smacks you in the spirit when you ride a wave: the incredible power of the sea. You are riding tornadoes that are lying on their side. You're a flea on a sleeping, snoring dinosaur. You're riding a god, or the horses of the gods. It feels supernatural.

It's more than riding a horse, even a stallion; it's like riding a steam locomotive. It's locomotion on the ocean. You feel the wave's great, grinding driving wheels beneath you just like on a steam engine. Is it mere coincidence that the word that means "to heat up the boiler of a steam engine" is also "stoke"?!

But this locomotive isn't a machine – it's alive. So it's more like a giant horse. But of course you don't really *ride* a wave as you ride a horse. You have to tame a horse before you ride it, but you can never tame a wave. You *catch* a wave as a catcher catches a curve ball from the pitcher.

Maybe the thrill in stoke is not just in the

power but also in the *danger*. For millions of years, no human being on earth ever even dared to *think* of riding those monsters. Waves can kill you. Failure doesn't mean death in baseball, or basketball, or golf, but failure can mean death in surfing.

But death cannot dish out any thrills, only life can, especially life at the edge, at the beach, where land and sea, life and death, touch each other.

As life is deepest and best where it touches death, land-based life is deepest and best where it touches the sea. What death does to life, sea does to land. The landlubber looks at the surfer and says, "He's gone from the land of the living." But the surfer looks back at the land and says, "I was never really alive there, I'm only alive here."

* * * * *

But is stoke really mystical?

Three or four millennia ago, India discovered that a supra-rational state of blissful consciousness could be attained by a lifetime of arduous yoga and meditation. A few centuries ago, Polynesia and Hawaii discovered that something like it could be attained by good athletes after long practice on a surfboard. Then in the 20th century California discovered that it could be attained instantly by anyone on a boogie board: instant, harmless Nirvana for the masses.

But what is it? How does it work?

The same way as ordering a hot dog: "Make me one with everything." No, I mean that seriously:

(1) It makes you one with the wave,

(2) and the wave is one with the sea, for a wave is simply the whole sea waving at you,

(3) and the sea is the perfect concrete symbol for Everything ("the ocean of Being"),

(4) so surfing makes you one with Everything.

All the mystics agree that you simply cannot explain the experience in words. So let me try. (Fools rush in where mystics fear to tread.) It's really quite simple:

Fact #1: When you're in a wave, your body becomes part of the wave.

Fact #2: What your body does, your soul does too. You're not two people but one. That's why your soul feels liquid and mobile and light in a wave. It's no longer a landlocked soul. It's not made of solid earth any more. It's more like a wave than like a thing. And it sees its own reflection in the water. The sea is its mirror, in which it knows itself.

(So surfing teaches you to "know thyself."

Surfing is Socratic.)

Now put these two facts together. If your body is one with the wave and your soul is one with your body, then your soul is one with the wave.

And that means that you're "in" a wave not as a sardine is "in" a can but as your soul is "in" your body. You *are* your body. You can't take it off, like your clothes. And you can't take the sea off your soul either because even after you come out of the water, the water never comes out of you.

* * * * *

There's a scientific basis for this feeling of becoming one with everything when you become one with the wave. For everything conspired to make this one wave, everything from the Big Bang through the death of the dinosaurs to last night's storm. Surfing is always global: the sea horses we ride have run through every field of water on earth. The water we touch has flowed under Antarctic icebergs and round tropical islands, through Norwegian fjords and California kelp fields, around Manhattan Island and uninhabited atolls, Saragasso calms and hundred-foot-high waves at Cape Horn. The water we ride is a world traveler. It comes from everywhere.

But "everywhere" has a *character*. It's not an

abstraction but a living, breathing, pumping reality. You feel this reality in the waves, and in birth, and in death, and in the sun. It's incredibly strong, and it's breathing, *right now, here,* in everything that exists. Existing is an *act.* "Being" is a verb, not a noun. Be-ing is what bees do. With apologies to Dylan Thomas, "the force that through the green fuse drives the flower / drives my red blood" *and also drives the blue wave and my board on it.* It's the Tao, of course, the energy of life itself, the blood of the universe, the pulse of the cosmic Mother. There's a soul in it. When you come to know it, you want to shout, "Look out! It's alive!" The Iroquois call it *Orenda.* It's why we love air and sky, trees and mountains, sea and stars. It's the mystical sugar God put in all these things to make them taste so sweet.

I think we all secretly long to get *inside* these great powers and beauties of nature that we see. Looking at them from the outside is already wonderful enough to make you cry, but getting *in* – that would be truly mystical. Well, surfers get in.

Everyone loves to look at crystals – diamonds, snow, ice – but surfers can slide inside their crystals. The "Green Room," the tube inside the wave, is a collapsing crystal cathedral made of water. You can enter, ride, and exit this inner sanctum untouched. No, that's wrong, you never exit untouched. You have been touched, deeply touched, touched by the finger of God.

It's the "being *in*" that's the thrill. It's like the difference between being in a great choir and listening to it from afar. Surfing is going inside nature's music.

Music is waves too, waves of sound. Music and water are different matter but a common form. Pythagoras taught that the planets made music, "the music of the spheres." He said we didn't hear it because we were too close to it, we were part of the music, since the earth is one of the "spheres" (planets). That's how it is with the sound of the surf: after you live on the shoreline for years, you don't notice the sound of the surf even though you hear it all the time. You don't notice it *because* you hear it all the time. You don't notice it for the same reason you don't notice yourself. It has actually become part of yourself, or you have become part of it.

Perhaps the best word for this mystical relation to the sea is "melt." You melt and flow into it like a butter patty on a hot pile of mashed potatoes. You soften. You get very humble. "Melting" also means getting hot, even if the water is cold, because you are in the eye of the energy hurricane. Finally, "melting" also means disappearing, dying. But that death is good, supremely good. It's the death of the caterpillar to release the butterfly.

Every surfer has a dream of riding the Ultimate Wave, a gigantic green juggernaut that annihilates everything. But this wave is not Death but Life – or maybe it's both.

Paradoxically, you come to be only after you die. The "I" is a phoenix. The only way to find your self is to lose it.

The "bottom line" is that "to surf" is not just something you do but something you are. I surf, therefore I am.

* * * * *

Most mystics are religious, though most religious believers are not mystics. Surfing is religious, but it's not a religion. If it is one, it's not an organized religion but a disorganized religion. Come to think of it, I've never seen an "organized religion." They all look pretty disorganized to me. Surfing is "religious" as Noah's ark is religious: can you imagine "organizing" all those animals?

The old Hawaiians attached spiritual significance to surfing, and I do not classify this as super-stition. The Hawaiian priest, the "big Kahuna," uttered religious incantations over the making of the sacred surfboard because they saw surfing as a sacred sign signifying something somehow super-natural. (Sorry for all those S's, but that's the shape of a wave, after all.) What is a "sacred sign"? It's like a handkerchief dropped by a goddess, or like a beam of starlight from another world. The tube of a breaking wave is called "the green cathedral" not because it *looks* like a cathedral but because it *feels* like one. You get that religious sense of awe inside. Time stops. You stop breathing. You are total attention. Because you know this is a magic door where the fundamental force of all nature, wave energy, is now breaking through into our little world. Where does it come from? What's on the other side of that door? See? Those are religious questions. Surfing doesn't give you religious answers – it doesn't tell you whether to be a Christian or a Muslim or a Buddhist – but it does give you religious questions.

I don't claim to know what God is, but I think I know two things God isn't: *bad* and *boring*. Waves are like God that way: they're *good*, but they're not boring because they're not *tame*. They're like

Aslan. Most things in life strike us as either good and boring or evil and interesting. "He lived another day" is good but boring. "He died today" is interesting but bad. But surfing is not bad and not boring, and that makes it Godlike.

Like religion, surfing is totally impractical. It doesn't make you rich[3] or powerful or famous (unless you become a surf prostitute). All it gives you is joy. See? – it's Godlike that way too. God doesn't give a damn about being rich or famous or powerful. That's why He says we shouldn't either. He preaches what He practices. He doesn't *need* us any more than the sea does. All He does is *give* Himself to us, give us splashes of His joy and beauty and power – as the sea does.

When King David the psalm writer needed a symbol for God, he turned naturally to the sea. "The floods have lifted up, O Lord, / The floods have lifted up their voice. / The floods lift up their waves. / The Lord on high is mightier than the noise of many waters, / Yea, than the mighty waves of the sea." (Psalm 93) And the other prophets did the same: "Thou didst walk through the sea with Thy horses, / Through the heap of great waters." (Habakkuk 3:15) But how often did David or

3 But see point 8, pp. 68 ff. It *can*.

Habakkuk see great waves? How often did they even see the sea? The only sea they ever saw was the Mediterranean. How often does the Mediterranean have great waves? Did they ever hold an international surfing championship in Israel? David probably had a once-in-a-lifetime experience of seeing great storm waves, and the image haunted his dreams and stuck in his spirit so deeply that he repeatedly used *that* image in his psalms as a natural symbol for God. (That really makes me want to meet God!)

I think God surfs all the time. What surfboards does He use? Us. He shapes His boards (us) through everything that happens to us. The shaping tools are the whole universe. And each board is unique, not mass-produced.

I think we surf in God too, not just in Heaven (see the poem on pages 54–55) but on earth right now. We live in three oceans. There is the one we surf in, which is below us (if we are above sea level). Above us is another ocean, made of air. We surf this every minute by breathing. Third, above the sky, above the whole universe, there is another ocean, an ocean of invisible joy. God is that ocean. We learn to surf on His waves upside down. And that's the meaning of life. Following the wave of

Ultimate Reality, riding the swells of Divine Providence, ecstatically surrendering to the foaming joy of God – that's the mystical essence of every good religion on earth, and that's the life of Heaven, and that's surfing.

Reason #3: Because It Make You Peaceful (Confucius and Lao Tzu)

(Surfing as Surrender: Soul-Surfing vs. Competitive Surfing)

Confucius and Lao Tzu were the two greatest philosophers in the history of the world's largest country, China. They could be called either philosophers or founders of religions, since religion and philosophy are not sharply distinguished in the East, as they are in the modern West. They were contemporaries; in fact they were the only two founders of religions that ever met each other. Their styles are complete opposites: formal vs. informal, rational vs. intuitive, societal vs. individualistic, large vs. small, organized vs. disorganized, city vs. country, artificial vs. natural. Yet they have one thing in common: for both, the key value is peace through harmony with nature. (Nature here means not the sum total of material things but the way things are, the force that moves the "ten thousand things under heaven.")

One philosophy of surfing, "soul-surfing," is the perfect sacrament, or art, or icon, of the peace that both Confucius and Lao Tzu taught. Soul-surfing gives you the deep, peaceful "stoke" that both Confucians and Taoists seek and find in other, more landlocked, ways.

There are two kinds of "stoke," and they are not just different but polar opposites. They are generated by two opposite kinds of surfing, which in turn flow from two opposite philosophies of life, two opposite relationships to all of reality, and to nature, and to the sea, and to the wave. One ("soul-surfing") is the psychological essence of all religion: peace through surrender. The other (competition) is the opposite, and is the essential psychological criticism of all religion as "passive" and "dehumanizing"; it is the essential secular alternative to all religion.

I'm not saying there are only two kinds of surfers, or that every one fits simply into one class or the other. The two kinds of surfing are two Platonic Forms, two ideals, two philosophies. Almost all surfers (both on the sea and on life) combine in themselves elements of both types, in different proportions. But almost everyone is predominantly of one type rather than the other.

One type I call macho-surfing. It's competitive. Its slanguage is full of violence: "rip," "shred," "tear." Its philosophy is the philosophy of Hitler, and Nietzsche, and Napoleon. The philosophy of the other kind of surfing, "soul-surfing," is the philosophy of Gandhi, and Buddha, and Jesus, as well as Confucius and Lao Tzu.

Macho-surfing is an ego-trip. Soul-surfing is a way to *lose* your ego, or at least your ego-consciousness. The macho-surfer surfs to show off; the soul-surfer surfs to show off *the wave*. The macho-surfer surfs to conquer; the soul-surfer surfs to be conquered. The macho-surfer thinks waves exist for surfers; the soul-surfer thinks surfers exist for waves. The macho-surfer wants to humanize the ocean; the soul-surfer wants to oceanize humanity.

The macho-surfer gets his stoke from conquest, from making the Big Wet Bitch submit, like a sadist. He gets his stoke when he feels like God – a certain kind of God, anyway: macho-God, The God with the Big Fist, Shiva the Destroyer. The soul-surfer gets his stoke from feeling like the opposite kind of God: the God who gives life: Vishnu,

Buddha, Christ, the God who likes to be anonymous and invisible, the God who dies to Himself.

The macho-surfer is like the letter I, a pillar of ego; or the letter A, a slave-built pyramid, hard and straight and cold as a rock. The soul-surfer is like the letter S: like a wave, soft and round and warm and womblike. The macho-surfer's guru is Atilla the Hun. The soul-surfer's guru is Lao Tzu. The *Tao-Te-Ching* is the Bible of soul-surfing.

Lao Tzu would have made a great surfer. His advice for life is advice for surfing because Tao is like the sea. Dance with it but let it lead. Ride it, don't fight it. Be relaxed, not rigid. Paint with the grain, not against it. Don't try to carry it, let it carry you. It's neither your slave nor your slave-master. Don't assert yourself and you will find yourself. Die to yourself and you will live. Disappear: that gives you the highest stoke of all, for that's what Tao does. Yield, even to riptide. Especially to riptide; that's the only way to survive it. "Resist not the evil one." Fight it, and you will lose. Don't fight it, and you will win. "If you don't contend, no one can contend against you." "What if they gave a war and nobody came?" Practice *wei-wu-wei*, "doing by not doing." Practice *islam*, surrender.

This "surrender" is *not* passive, any more than a

woman is passive sexually. She is *receptive*, both physically and spiritually. She is *responsive*.

It's like education. The word "docile" means literally "teachable." But a sheep, or a blackboard, is not teachable because it is passive. Docility (teachability) means just the opposite of passivity. Learning is an activity, not a passivity. A piece of paper or a computer bank is passive, but a mind is active.

To receive, mentally or physically, is an act. Ask any catcher. And catching a wave is even more active than catching a baseball.

The ancient Romans had a great way of describing an uneducated person: they said, "He had neither learned to read nor to swim." The sea is a great book; learn to read it. Don't "shred" it or "tear" it or "rip" it, like an infant or an animal, trying to read the book with its teeth.

If you surrender to this wave of Tao, you *become* it, and then you become as active and as powerful as the wave because you now *are* the wave, or a part of it, or *in* it. You're not sitting on it like a rodeo cowboy and trying to tame it. That's the very last thing you want to do: tame it!

Life is like an unstoppable wave that comes to us with irresistible force. We should not try to be immovable objects. The irresistible force defeats the immovable object. Hurricanes blow down oak trees, but not willows, which bend in the wind.

There are sections of London that were bombed to rubble in World War II and not repaired for years. And what did we see years later in those piles of rubble? Grass. The grass pushed the concrete aside and cracked it. Grass is stronger than concrete because it's alive. Waves are stronger than rocks because they're alive. The waves of life are always stronger than the rigid objects of death.

The reason life comes in waves is because life gets its form from its mother, and all life comes from mother ocean. Literally. If there were no ocean there would be no life on earth, none at all, anywhere. Listen to your mother. Mothers know life. Mothers *give* life.

"Surrender" to the sea is not just loss of control. It's that, but it's also gaining control at the same time. For you have become water, and now you know how to flow serenely and powerfully at the same time. You are both strong and gentle. The macho man's mistake is not his love of strength and power. His mistake is his assumption that he has to choose either strength *or* gentleness, and his assumption that surrender to Tao is weakness instead of strength. But it takes strength to surrender. Not many people have the strength to do that.

Here is a proof of the fact that you probably do not have the strength to surrender. Meditation is mental surrender, surrendering your conscious mind's control. Do you find it easy to do that? Can you stay alone and totally silent for fifteen minutes? Or does it take too much strength, too much mental energy for you? It's a *calm, quiet* energy, and it doesn't drain you and make you tired, but it is *energy*. It is activity, not passivity.

The two surfing styles are also two whole lifestyles, for life is like an ocean, and everything in life comes in waves, and there are two ways of surfing them. Macho surfing on the waves of life sees living (and surfing) as a kind of technology, and success as some kind of technique, a method, a way of making the Other submit to the Ego. Sometimes the macho-surfer-on-life even applies this to *people*. He wants to tame them into affectionate pets. "Down, boy!" is his word to the other. The soul surfer doesn't say to the wave: "Down, boy!" He says: "Up, girl!"

Fortunately, most surfers aren't good enough to be professional competitive surfers and become surf prostitutes, surfing for money, just as most baseball players and basketball players aren't good enough to play professionally, but only for the love of the game. So most surfers are soul-surfers.

And all surfers start out that way. If they didn't love surfing for its own sake to begin with, they wouldn't begin to surf, and if they don't begin to surf, they can't later become surf prostitutes. Similarly, most sex prostitutes start out having sex for love, or at least for fun, before they get corrupted into doing it for money.

The surfing magazines that feature and foster surfing competitions are a little bit like pornography. "Surf competitions" make about as much sense as "sex competitions." Surfing is not a business. Business is naturally competitive, but surfing is more like a religion than like a business. Can you imagine religious mystics competing with each other for the best mystical experience, and doing it for money?

Surrender is essential to religion. But each religion produces both saints and sinners. Islam, the religion whose very name means "surrender," fosters both great saints and mystics (many of them are Sufis) and also great warlords and terrorists. I know there are Sufi surfers (I met one), and I'll bet no one in Al Qaeda surfs.

Reason #4: Because It Makes You Good (Moses)
(The Ten Commandments of the Sea)

Surfing is not an organized religion; it's more like a disorganized religion. But it's not so disorganized that it has no commandments. In fact, it has ten, and they are very similar to the ten you already know from Moses (or rather from God through Moses):

1. Have no gods before Me.
2. Make no graven images.
3. Do not take the name of the Lord in vain.
4. Remember the Sabbath.
5. Honor your father and mother.
6. Do not kill.
7. Do not steal.
8. Do not commit adultery.
9. Do not lie.
10. Do not covet.

The sea teaches us these commandments too, in its own way:

1. Surrender to the Creator of the sea. Know your weakness by knowing the sea's power. Know your ignorance by knowing the sea's mystery. Know your smallness by knowing the sea's greatness. Remember the prayer of the Normandy sailor: "O Lord, my board is so small and Your sea is so big." (Keep it short and simple like that.) The sea is the biggest thing we can see on earth. It is thus a natural icon for God's greatness, and, correlatively, for our smallness and for the wisdom of humility.

2. Do not worship even the biggest, most beautiful thing on earth, the sea. Only God is God. Do not confuse the finite with the Infinite.

And do not look to the sea instead of God for morality. The sea has no morality. It kills. It steals. It deceives. It dishonors. It will wash away your sorrows, and it will wash away your shallowness, but it will not wash away your sins.

3. Listen to the sea. It will teach you to listen more and to speak less. It will teach you not to take names in vain.

Listen to the sea so that you can learn to listen

better. Learn to listen better so that you can listen to God. Listen to God so that you can listen to other people. Listen to other people so that you can know yourself. "Know thyself" by listening to the sea.

4. Let the sea teach you to forget time and to just *be*. Let it teach you that there is never any good reason to rush until Grandma falls into the deep end of the swimming pool. Until then let the sea teach you to celebrate Sabbaths. "Near the sea, we forget to count the days."

5. Honor your ancestors' honor of the sea, and their honor of all nature. They saw nature as the cathedral given to you by your Creator, loaded with icons like the sea to remind you to surrender to Him. They honored nature; they didn't try to conquer her. Don't try to conquer your mother.

6. Do not kill nature. Do not kill the sea. She is your mother. Take care of your mother. Use your power to save your mother from ugliness-pollution.

Do not kill beauty. Beauty is your soul's life,

your soul's water. You need beauty more than you need power or wealth or even knowledge. Use power and wealth and knowledge to preserve beauty.

7. Do not adulterate the sea. Preserve her purity, and yours. Do not sell her, or use her. Love her, and all God's gifts. Use and sell *your* creations; love and appreciate God's. Adulterate nothing; treat everything as what it is.

8. Do not steal; be grateful for what you have. God has given you the world's best and biggest toy: the sea. Play in it. Let it teach you cosmic gratitude for the whole ocean of being, which contains so many fish. Gratitude is the clearest hallmark of wisdom.

9. Do not lie. Be what you are. Be as sincere as sea water. Rehearse for eternity: be simple. Be.

10. Do not believe the lies of covetousness, or greed, or lust. Do not believe our culture's pervasive superstition that you can solve every problem by *doing* something about it. The sea is not a problem to be solved but a mystery to be enjoyed. The

sea is like life that way. It is also like life in that it possesses nothing but gives all things, gives all life-forms. Be like the sea: be a giver, not a grabber.

Reason #5: Because It Makes You Christ-like (Jesus)
(The Cross as a Surfboard)

In California I met one of the "Jesus people" left over from the Sixties who proved to me that Jesus was the world's greatest surfer.

First, he walked on water.

Then, for three years he duck-dived through the waves that were trying to wipe him out.

Finally, he got out his longboard in the shape of an old rugged cross.

He waxed his board with nails.

Two men named Simon went surfing with him. One, from Cyrene, helped him carry his cross-board out. The other, from Galilee, deserted him and returned to shore when Satan raised some big waves. (The Bible calls Satan "the prince of the power of the air," and it's the power of the air that raises waves.)

His last wave was enormous. He caught it with perfect timing, right on the curl. He rode the tube, the Red Room, while bleeding in five places and surrounded by sharks.

Then he crouched to prone and came out the other end of the tube standing upright.

Then he beckoned you aboard his board: "Will you come surfing with me?"

And Jesus was a sailor
When he walked upon the water
And he spent a long time watching
From his lonely wooden tower
And when he knew for certain
Only drowning men could see him
He said "All men will be sailors then
Until the sea shall free them."

And you want to travel with him
And you want to travel blind
And you think maybe you'll trust him
For he's touched your perfect body with his mind.

("Suzanne" by Leonard Cohen)

Reason #6: Because It Makes You Heavenly (Plato)
(Surfing in Heaven)

The most influential philosopher in history is Plato. "Plato is philosophy and philosophy is Plato," said Emerson. "The best way to summarize the history of Western philosophy would be as a series of footnotes to Plato," said Whitehead.

Plato's one "big idea," the idea that defines Platonism, is the idea of "Platonic Ideas" or "Platonic Forms." These are not ideas in our minds, but objectively real essences that are perfect and eternal. Everything we know is a pale imitation of them. They are archetypes, perfect models. We use them to judge imperfect things. For instance, we judge lines as more or less straight insofar as they approach the perfectly straight line, which no one has ever seen. (All visible lines, when sufficiently magnified, turn out to be a little crooked.) According to Plato, every dog is a shadow or copy of The Perfect Dog, or Perfect Dogginess. Every human being we know is partly human and partly inhuman; only in Heaven will we be perfect, that is, perfectly human, perfectly ourselves.

Where are these Ideas? Nowhere in this world, but in Heaven. When we get there, after death, we will know them, contemplate them, conform to them, become one with them eternally. Then we will reach our perfection. Everything on earth is a pale shadow of something in Heaven. Everything here is a foretaste, a rehearsal, an appetizer of something There.

This idea is also found in the New Testament (though the writers of the New Testament were not Platonists). According to Christianity, life on earth and in time is a preparation for life in Heaven and in eternity.

St. Augustine, four centuries after Christ, said there was one thing lacking in Plato: a home for the Platonic Ideas. Ideas don't exist in nothing, or in space, or in matter, but in minds. But no human mind is perfect and eternal, So the Ideas must exist in the Mind of God. Augustine thus married Platonic philosophy and Biblical religion at their center.

Now if you combine this Platonic idea with the Biblical idea, inherited from Judaism and taken over by Christianity, that there is a single God who alone is all-perfect, and that our ultimate eternal destiny is some kind of union, or communion, or spiritual marriage, with God, what do you get? You get the conclusion below, which is an original poem that is a commentary on a quotation from the Book of Revelation, the last book of the New Testament, about what will and will not be in Heaven. The point of the poem is that it is surfing that best explains the quotation. You could also make the same point by saying that the quotation is the best explanation of surfing.

(The quotation:) "Then I saw a new heaven and a new earth. For the first heaven and the first earth had passed away, and there was no more sea. . . . And one of the angels . . . showed me the holy city, Jerusalem, coming down out of heaven from God. . . . I did not see any temple in the city, for the Lord God almighty and the Lamb are its temple. . . . The city does not need the sun or the moon to shine in it, for the glory of God gives it light." (Revelation 21: 1, 9–10, 22–23)

"Surfing in Heaven"

When come new heavens and new earth,
This world will be but afterbirth.
For every earthly thing is leaven
To fertilize the bread of Heaven.
Yet every glorious thing created
Shall shine in that world unabated,
And each beloved bird and beast
Will be there at the wedding feast.
And all the art that men have made
Will at His holy feet be laid.

Yet in those perfect Heavenly places
There seem to be three empty spaces.
For Revelation Twenty-one
Mentions three things whose life is done.
In Heaven three things will not be:
No sun, no temple, and no sea.
Now we are told the deeper cause
For two of these apparent flaws:

(1) The Temple Mount, in all its parts,
Imaged the One who'd dwell in hearts.
With Bridegroom here, His wineglass token
Is now fulfilled by being broken.

(2) There's no sun in that new creation
But that too is an affirmation:
The Son of God will be our sun,
And moon, and stars, when time is done.
So will the heavenly solar sight
Prove Aken-Aton almost right.

(3) The reason for no heavenly sea
Must be the same, it seems to me:
As He's our temple and our sun,
He'll be our sea when life is done.
When this old body lies in sod,
My soul shall body-surf in God.

Reason #7: Because It Makes You Sexy
(Freud)
(Why Surfing Is Better than Sex)

Everybody knows one thing about Freud, the founder of modern psychology: that he discovered that just about everything was about sex (though he did once famously say that "sometimes a cigar is just a cigar"). Whatever else he may have said that was true or false, and whether or not his "discoveries" were as original as he and his followers thought (many of them can be found in Book 9 of Plato's *Republic)*, this is sure to be his lasting legacy.

But Freud never surfed. Suppose he had?

Jean-Luc was a Frenchman whom I met on Second Beach at Newport, Rhode Island. I was alternating body-surfing with bodyboarding, while he was hot-dogging on a spiffy red shortboard. His friend Andre, a non-surfer, watched from the beach. Jean-Luc introduced me to Andre, and then the two of them had the following argument. I think they were showing off for me because I had introduced myself to them as a philosopher, and they were trying to be philosophical. I'm "festooning" the actual conversation only a little bit in what follows.

Jean-Luc was trying to convince Andre to try surfing for the first time by the one argument that is supposed to settle everything for a Frenchman: "It is supremely sexy."

"Ridiculous," said Andre.

"I will prove this ridiculous thing to you."

"How?"

"Scientifically. By statistics."

"What statistics?"

"A poll. There was a poll of surfers around the world – I think it was a hundred – you should have read about it; it was in the papers only a little while ago – and this poll, you see, it asked surfers to choose between sex and surfing. The question was this: If you had to give up either sex or surfing for the rest of your life, which would you give up?"

"And what were the results?"

"Eighty nine chose to give up sex. Eleven chose to give up surfing."

"Impossible. I do not believe it."

"Neither did the surfers who wrote in to the magazine. They said they couldn't believe anyone could find eleven surfers who would give up surfing."

"Ha! It is a funny story, yes? But it is only a poll. It proves nothing. It explains nothing."

"Would you like me to explain it to you?"

"Please."

"Then imagine making such love that the thrill is not just in one organ of your body but in every cell of your body. Would that not be better?"

"Of course."

"Now imagine you can keep doing it all day without getting bored."

"A twelve-hour orgasm?"

"Yes. And now imagine making this kind of love not just to one woman but to every woman in the world . . ."

"That would take too long."

". . . at the same time!"

"What an imagination you have!"

"No, I have just imagined surfing."

"You are exaggerating."

"No. I am imagining. And I have another analogy for you, Andre. Have you ever felt the shock of an astonishingly beautiful girl looking at you and smiling at you?"

"I have indeed."

"Fortunate mortal! Then you know. Tell me what you know. Tell me how it feels in that moment."

"It feels like . . . like everything has stopped. Time has stopped. You do not breathe. The whole world stands still. Nothing happens. And yet, at that same moment, your heart is pounding like a locomotive. For something momentous is happening, something *formidable*."

"That is exactly right, Andre – and that is exactly the feeling of catching a great wave. The thrill comes from the same combination: awesome grandeur and playful intimacy. Her smile means that this magnificent creature is inviting your spirit to enter into her spirit, and into her happiness, for one split second."

Andre turned to me. "Is this true?"

"Yes," I said.

"You too have fallen in love, I see," said Andre.

"You can fall in love over and over again in the waves," I replied. Jean-Luc was nodding vigorously.

Andre did not answer, but he looked thoughtful.

Andre was very intelligent but also very strange. He then started to defend "just watching" rather than actually surfing, and did it quite eloquently by identifying himself with the English Victorians. "The Victorians did not surf," he said, "but no one ever loved the sea more than they did. They were happy just to see and smell the sea. They were contemplatives. Like Dante contemplating Beatrice. They did not want to *invade* her."

I protested: "But when you contemplate a beautiful mystery of nature, don't you long to enter it? Don't you feel tragically alienated from it, looking in from the outside, like a homeless bum at a royal ball? If you know the Romantic poets, you know they all felt that way. Well, you can overcome that tragic alienation from nature by surfing. You can get *in*."

"One of them did that," Andre replied. "Byron. He drowned."

Perhaps Andre was just a coward, I thought.

Later in the day, the three of us left the beach at the same time. The tide was very high, and the waves were sloshing and foaming against the rocks beside the parking lot road. "Look," Jean-Luc said to Andre, pointing to the waves. "It is having an orgasm."

"Is it true, as they say, that to a Frenchman *everything* means sex?" I asked, jokingly.

"No," Jean-Luc replied, seriously. "But anyone can see that *that* does. Just look: the sea is trying to stand outside itself, to escape itself, to have an ecstasy, to become one with the land. It is pouring itself out on the rocks as a man pours out his life into a woman."

I was amazed at Andre's reply. "No, Jean-Luc. The sea is not a metaphor for sex. Both the sea and sex are a metaphor for something else."

"And what is that?"

"Mystical love. That is what Allah is: self-transcending ecstasy." (Andre was a Sufi Muslim.)

"You are a heretic, Andre. Your Qur'an never says that Allah has ecstasy."

"Oh, but it does. In fact, this is the word the Holy Qur'an uses the most often for Allah: 'the Merciful.' That is His ecstasy. Mercy is His ecstasy. *Allah akbar!*"

From that day on, I could never again see that white foam without thinking of the divine mercy.

When I discovered how Andre loved the sea and the English Romantic poets, and that he was a Sufi Muslim, I asked him, "Do you ever feel guilty about loving the Romantic poets too much, or loving the sea too much?" (I asked this for personal reasons. As a Christian, I fear idolatry as much as a Muslim does.) Andre's answer proved to me that he was a real mystic: "Before I became a Sufi, I did feel this guilt. I was torn by two separate loves, like a husband who falls in love with another woman while still loving his wife. But when I became a Sufi, I discovered that the two women I loved were the same woman, in disguise. Can you imagine how that discovery felt?"

"No."

"Yes, you can. Go ahead. Imagine it. Tell me what you think."

"OK. I imagine you felt a tremendous relief to your conscience."

"Ah, you Americans. You think so much of conscience. Yes, I suppose I did feel that – though as a Frenchman I feel a little guilty confessing it. But the primary feeling was *excitement*. Can you imagine what an exciting discovery it is to find your lover in disguise?"

* * * * *

Thinking about this conversation, I decided that Jean-Luc was right about surfing being sexier than sex. Here are my reasons:

1. Most people can't remember their best

orgasm. But every surfer can remember his best wave.

2. Surfing is better than sex because it's a continuous orgasm in every cell of your body. It's a thousand little orgasms in a row, a million if you want, all day long, endless orgasms without ever having to stop to refuel (until you starve).

3. The sea is a woman to a man and a man to a woman. Here's how a female surfer describes it: "You're lying out there on your board. A swell approaches, like a man. You start to paddle toward the shore, pretending to flee, like a woman or a cat. It's teasing. It's foreplay. The wave comes right up to you singing 'Pretty Woman.' You tickle the wave's lip, then caress his face. He kisses you, says, 'It's time' – and you know it is. Time for climax. Time for you and him alone. You glide down his body. He thrusts himself at you. He thrusts his whole heavy body onto you. One part of it touches you. He thrusts his wetness at you: so white, so flowing, so foamy, so fast and turbulent. Then, suddenly, it's over and you're left gurgling with delight. I hope you don't think this is pornographic, because it's exactly what innocent little pre-pubescent kids do in waves."

4. Sex is also holy, because it's what Adam and

Eve did in Eden in obedience to God's first commandment, "Be fruitful and multiply." Do you think He meant: "Grow apples and memorize times tables"?

(The big difference between religious people and nonreligious people is that religious people have the category of 'the holy' and nonreligious people don't. So nonreligious people can't understand why religious people believe there are two kinds of anything, holy and unholy, including holy sex [faithful sex, giving your whole self, body and soul, in bed and out of it, to the one person you've given your whole life to] and unholy sex [unfaithful sex, sex with the rest of the world].)

5. Surfing gives you what each sex looks for in the other: strength and gentleness together. That's the supremely sexy combination that makes up the gentleman and the medieval knight, or the lady and Mother Nature. Whether you are a man or a woman, both you and the wave have to be both strong and gentle. It's a tricky combination, and it takes time and practice to learn it. If you're a man, you obviously have to be strong, but you also have to be gentle, for the trick is to go *with* the wave, not *against* it. It's dancing, not wrestling. And the wave is both strong and gentle too. You feel it lifting you

up as effortlessly as Big Mama lifts Tiny Baby. And if you're a woman, it must be even more obvious to you that you have to be strong and gentle at the same time.

6. Surfing is also like sex in this way: the primary thrill is not just physical but mental: it's the *intimacy*, the incredible knowledge that the Great Other is letting you into his/her inner sanctum. It feels like God personally inviting you into His Holy of Holies.

There is a spectrum of intimacy, from shortboard to longboard to bodyboard to body-surfing. The feeling of intimacy is greater the less you put in its way, the less you contracept. Sometimes even a surfboard feels like a condom and you want to just body-surf. Next best is the bodyboard, which plunges you down into the water rather than inviting you to stand up on your board like a circus acrobat on horseback or a Roman centurion whipping a prisoner with a whip. (Of course that's not the only feeling you get on a standup surfboard. That's a perversion, like rape, and rape is the farthest thing from sex: it's a denial of sex. Rape is monolithic power; sex is mutual surrender.)

The aim of love is intimacy, union, in fact the total union which is impossible yet irresistibly desirable. But though totally *perfect* union is impossible in this world, totally *unimpeded* union is not, if you insert no obstacle, mental or physical, to the total self-giving.

The same is true of surfing as of sex.

Sometimes a wetsuit feels like a condom. Granted, even surfing with a wetsuit can be an incredibly intimate thing, but it can't give you the complete high you can get from that totally natural experience of direct and complete sensory immersion you get when the hot sun caresses your skin and the cool water refreshes it and every pore feels every drop of water; when total body awareness brings about total soul awareness. You feel naked, defenseless, totally natural, and simple. It's totally sensual and totally spiritual at once. And totally innocent (until you pervert it). It overcomes the common but unnatural dualism between the spiritual and the sensual. You simply feel the simple fact of sheer existence and its bliss. And you feel it with your whole self, soul and body. This is life reduced to its essence. If this is not mystical, what is?

* * * * *

But the analogy is limited. For the sea is not a person, though it seems to be the icon of a Person (a divine person). And because the sea is not a person, surfing is not really better than sex. But it is an icon of something that *is* even better than sex, something that we will have in Heaven, something of which sex is also an icon.

Reason #8: Because It Can Make You Rich (Machiavelli)
(Five Surfing Lessons for Wall Street)

No, the title is not a misprint. Here is another conversation in the waves, this time in New England. It was October, and I was surfing small but perfectly formed waves at Nahant, Massachusetts, from a nor'easter that had just passed. The air was still wet, the sky was cloudy, the water was cold, and only two people were in the water: myself and a 35-year-old retired multimillionaire.

"How often do you surf here?" I asked him. (I don't know his name.)

"As often as I want."

"How can you afford to do that?"

"Oh, I'm retired."

"Retired? You can't be 40 years old."

"I'm 35. But I made enough money in ten years to retire for life."

"How? Did you inherit it?"

"Nope. Started from scratch."

"Did you invent something?"

"Nope. I played the stock market."

"You got lucky?"

"Not luck at all. I taught myself how to do it. And I learned it all from one great book."

"What book?"

"The one we're reading now."

"The ocean?"

"You got it. I learned the principles of financial success from surfing."

"Are you serious?"

"Dead serious."

"I'll bet you can guess my next question."

"You want me to list the principles?"

"Please."

"Glad to. There are five."

He held up one finger, keeping his eyes on the ocean. One of the most basic rules of surfing is Never Turn Your Back on the Ocean.

"One: practice with little waves first. Keep moving up to bigger ones.

"Two: learn to sense when the wave of opportunity is going to break, and catch it at the exact first moment it breaks. Timing is the key to everything. If you catch the opportunity wave too far out, it's too soon. If you rush it, you'll miss it. But if you wait and catch it too far in, you're late, and it's broken already and all you can do is catch the dinky foam, the little profits anybody can catch.

"Three: go out to meet the wave. Be proactive. Anticipate it. Feel it. Predict it. It takes practice, but calculation isn't enough, it takes feel. But to get that feel you have to be patient, you have to try over and over again, you have to watch long and hard. Waiting and watching is more than half the work. Like in painting. *Both* kinds of painting.

"Four: be fearless. Usually, the riskiest place to catch the wave is also the best place. You have to overcome your natural inclination to play it safe. You'll wipe out sometimes, but you'll also catch some humdingers that you'd never catch if you played it safe.

"Five: surf with a buddy for backup when the waves are big. You can save each other better than you can save yourself. And you can afford to take more chances if you know you have backup.

"And that's what worked for me. I surfed the market by the same rules I surfed the sea."

I was impressed. He may have been totally faking it, but it was a great story. I asked, "Did you also read books and take courses?"

"Oh, sure. But so did dozens of my friends, and none of them got as rich as me, because none of them surfed."

I can't certify that this guy was telling the truth. But I can certify that I am. I really had this conversation.

Reason #9: Because It Makes You Wise (Socrates)
(Surfing as the Antidote to Bullshit)

Here is a conversation I had with a fellow academic who found out that I was writing a book about surfing. Let's just call him Thomas (Doubting Thomas).

T: *writing* about surfing?
Me: Sure.
T: But surfers don't read. They surf.
Me: Right. It's pretty hard to read and surf at the same time, no matter what kind of board you use.
T: You know what I mean. Surfers are illiterate. Surf magazines are all pictures. The only other magazines like that are pornography. Surfers don't speak in sentences. And when they do, the sentences are never

more than seven words long, and the words
never have more than seven letters.

Me: Actually, there is one surf publication that
deliberately hews to that policy.

T: So I'm right. Surfers are deadheads, meatheads, or potheads.

Me: So which am I, then?

T: No, seriously, you're a professor, not a
surfer. You don't fit the mold.

Me: What mold? Define your terms!

T: You know what I mean. Surf culture.

Me: And how do you define surf culture?

T: You know.

Me: No I don't. That's why I'm asking you.

T: Sex and drugs and rock and roll. The "hey,
dude" scene. Do you have a different word
for surf culture?

Me: Yeah. I call it bullshit.[4]

T: So you're writing about bullshit?

Me: No, I'm writing about surfing, not surf culture. It's surf culture that's the bullshit. We
lay all this lifestyle bullshit and sex and

---

4 "Shit" is a good word. It's a good word because it's a good
thing, and it's a good thing because God created it. It's also
in the Bible: look up "dung" in a King James Version concor-
dance. See especially Philippians 3:8. Bulls are also good.
And two goods don't make a bad.

drugs and rock and roll bullshit and "hey, dude" bullshit and advertising bullshit and competition bullshit on surfing, *but it still survives.* Like the Catholic Church surviving the persecutions and the Dark Ages and the Black Death and the Spanish Inquisition and the Crusades and the Mafia popes and Galileo and the French Revolution and pedophile priests and spineless bishops. It's miraculous! Like the survival of the Jews, or like the ocean itself. All three survive our pollution because they're bigger than we are.

T: So you're writing about surfing, not surf culture.

Me: Yes. Writing about surf culture instead of surfing would be like writing about pollution in the ocean instead of the ocean. Come to think of it, that's what almost all the books about the ocean are about now. Just look in the bookstores. They're all about the problems and the pollution, not about the joy and the poetry and the love.

T: You should write a book like that about the

ocean too: one about the joy and the poetry and the love.

Me: I did. It's called *The Sea Within*.

T: Can you recommend another book about surfing but not about surf culture?

Me: All of them.

T: All of what?

Me: All books. All the great books are about surfing.

T: What in the world do you mean by that?

Me: All great books are about human life, and everything in life is like surfing, so all books are about surfing. For instance, take *The Man in the Iron Mask*. That shows you what it feels like to enter the ocean: to take off your iron mask, the one you wear on land. Or take *Dracula*. The surfer's soul sleeps in a coffin most of the time. Only when we come out to surf are we alive. Or take *Moby-Dick*. The *Pequod* is really only a very big surfboard. . . .

T: All right, already. I get the point. Everything is like surfing to the surfaholic.

Me: And do you know why?

T: No. Why?

Me: It's very logical. Everything is like surfing because surfing is like everything. Everything in the universe. It's the capstone of creation.

T: It's not logical and you know it. It's fanatical.

Me: It's perfectly logical, and I can prove it.

T: How?

Me: From the Bible. You accept that as proof, right? (T is an Evangelical.)

T: Yeah. How you going to do that?

Me: Wait here, and I'll show you.

At this point (we were in my home) I went down to the basement and emerged with an amateur videotape called "The Creation of the World." I popped it into the VCR. (This is not fiction. This is a real tape. It exists. I can tell you how to get it.) The music was a little tinny, and the pictures a little grainy, but T will never forget this tape. The title "The Seven Days of Creation" came on the screen for a few seconds, then silence and darkness. The music from "Thus Spake Zarathustra" began – the theme for the movie "2001."

"In the beginning . . . GOD" – and as soon as the word appeared on the screen, it suddenly changed from black to blinding light for a split

|second – "created the heavens and the earth." The Big Bang.

"And the earth was without form and void." A dark, heaving sea. No land.

"And the Spirit of God moved over the face of the waters." A dove, surfing on the air, making waves with its wings.

Each day of creation proceeded with arresting images. When God separated "the waters below" from "the waters above," two beautiful mirror images appeared: the night sea, flecked with white foam, and the night sky, flecked with white stars. Across the screen marched a long parade of strikingly varied plants, animals, birds, bugs, and fish, both normal and strange.

Then came creation's crowning moment: "And God created Man in His own image." Suddenly the screen filled with – Laird Hamilton on a forty foot wave!

T's smile was eloquent. He got the point.

"And that wasn't just 15 billion years ago, either," I reminded T.

"What do you mean by that?"

"I mean there's no such thing as an ex-surfer. Not even for God."

* * * * *

The Best Philosophy Lesson I Ever Taught

Not only is surfing not "hey, dude" brainlessness, it's philosophical. I teach philosophy, and I admire Socrates, its founder and archetype, and I think Socrates would have been proud of me for the following philosophy lesson, maybe the best one I ever taught.

There are two kinds of philosophy. Some philosophy is simply bullshit. Philosophers are smart, and therefore they can fool people pretty well. They are very clever at disguising bullshit as wisdom. The other kind of philosophy is really wise and wonderful and helpful. Socrates is my favorite example of it. If you don't know that both kinds of philosophy exist, you are not fully educated in philosophy.

There are three kinds of students. The first kind thinks all philosophy is bullshit. These students are not serious. They are cynical. The second kind thinks all philosophy is wisdom. These students are *too* serious. They are naïve. The third kind knows that some philosophy is bullshit and some is wisdom. They are "judgmental," and "discriminating" – which are two things our culture tells us not to be, so they are countercultural.

My job as a teacher of philosophy, as I see it, is

to get all students to see both the wisdom and the bullshit. That means making cynical students more serious and over-serious students more cynical, or at least more able to laugh at philosophy. The most satisfying part of my job is usually showing a little wisdom to the cynical students. But the best philosophy lesson I ever taught was the opposite: showing the bullshit to an over-serious student. (Yes, this has something to do with surfing. Be patient.)

I had this very smart, very serious student. Let's call him Smith. (I know two people whose first name is Smith.) Smith was totally in love with philosophy. It was his religion. He was going to save the world with it. I knew Smith would never be a great teacher if he remained over-serious. After taking his fourth straight straight-A course from me, he came to me with a worried look on his face and said he really needed to talk to me privately for a few minutes about the value of teaching philosophy, which he was planning to go into as a career. Since I thought it was not a good sign that he was so copycat dependent on me, I thought it *was* a good sign that he was questioning it all now.

So I took him to my new office. We had just moved into much plusher and larger quarters, and

I had just filled four enormous floor-to-ceiling bookcases with my books. He had never seen my new office before. He was impressed.

And here was my lesson. "Smith," I said, "you ask me what is the value of all this, right?" I gestured with both arms to the plethora of books.

"Exactly," Smith replied.

"Well, I think I am in a position to answer your question. I have been teaching this stuff full time for over forty years now. I have read at least a good part of every single one of these books, and many more besides that aren't here. Look: here we have the complete works of Homer, Hesiod, Aeschylus, Sophocles, Euripides, Plato, Aristotle, Plotinus, Marcus Aurelius, Justin Martyr, Augustine, Boethius, Aquinas, Machiavelli, Luther, Calvin, Descartes, Pascal, Hobbes, Spinoza, Leibnitz, Locke, Berkeley, Hume, Kant, Fichte, Hegel, Kierkegaard, Nietzsche, Marx, James, Dewey, Wittgenstein, Russell, Whitehead, Heidegger, Sartre, Marcel, Freud, Jung, Toynbee, Dawson, Gilson, Maritain, twelve different translations of the Bible, the *Koran*, the *Tao-Te-Ching*, the *Analects* of Confucius, the *Vedas*, the *Upanishads*, the *Bhagavad-Gita*, the *Dhammapada*, the *Shobogenzo*, the complete works of G.K.

Chesterton, C.S. Lewis, and Tolkien. Secondary sources, and secondary sources on secondary sources. Big books, little books, dull books, interesting books, true books, false books. So I think I'm in a position to answer your question about the value of philosophy."

Smith was impressed. He sat down, without being asked to.

"So here is my judgment about what it all means, in one word." Smith was all ears. "It's bullshit, Smith, it's an enormous pile of bullshit."

Smith looked as if he was about to die. It took him at least six shocked seconds to find his voice. "But Professor, you're the best philosophy teacher I ever met, and this is your life's work. You gave your life to this, and you're still doing it. How can you call it bullshit? How can you go on? What keeps you going? If this is not the meaning of life for you, what is?"

It was exactly the question I had hoped he would ask. "I will not tell you, Smith. I will do something better than that. I will show you. I will *show* you the meaning of life."

Smith's eyes and ears both doubled in size. I reached behind my large, messy desk and pulled out the meaning of life: a yellow boogie board. (An old

Challenger Kauai Classic.) "This is the meaning of life, Smith. This is the meaning of life. Surfing is the meaning of life." My smile was like the sun.

It was a risk. Smith could have spat at me, or shaken his head and wobbled away, but instead he laughed, at first hesitatingly, then uncontrollably. We both did, together, for about thirty seconds. My serious, worrisome colleague in the office across the hall heard us and thought we had gone insane.

"You've never tried it? Not even on a boogie board?"

"No."

"Try it. You'll like it." I was in the old Alka-Seltzer commercial. "And it will make you a better philosopher."

"Why?"

"Because it will make you loose."

"Why is loose good?"

"Was it good to laugh, just now?"

"Very good."

"That was being loose."

"Oh."

"You took logic. So draw the logical conclusion. Logic isn't bullshit, you know."

I don't know whether Smith ever got into surfing, but I think he got into being more human. And I think I may have added ten years to his life.

(Note: After teaching this lesson, and thinking it was brilliantly original, I remembered two sources I had unconsciously copied. One was an episode of the old "Bob Newhart Show" and the other was the story about St. Thomas Aquinas, who refused to complete his masterpiece the *Summa Theologica* because he had a mystical experience shortly before he died, and when asked why he wrote no more answered, "Because compared with what I have seen, everything I have ever written looks to me like nothing but straw." The Greek word *skubala*, used in Philippians 3:8, can mean dung, garbage, ashes, or straw.)

Reason #10: Because Anyone Can Do It (George Morey)

What? George Morey up there with the great philosophers?

For one of the greatest inventions of all time: the boogie board. ("Bodyboard" is the correct term, but "boogie board" is the affectionate "pet name.")

Why is that one of the greatest inventions of all time?

Because bodyboarding *is* surfing, and *everybody* can bodyboard, therefore everybody can surf – all because of George Morey.

The Bodyboard and the Printing Press

Reading books is one of life's great pleasures. A book is a hole in the world. Reading a book is like jumping down Alice's rabbit hole and entering a new world, a wonderland.

But before Gutenberg invented movable type and the printing press, all books were written out by hand, and copied by hand, and therefore so rare and expensive that only the elite few could afford to own them. Five hundred years ago, Gutenberg took this elitist pleasure and democratized it. Now everyone can afford books.

Fifty years ago, George Morey did the same thing to surfing.

Morey democratized stoke. He made surfing available not only to the young, strong, athletic few but to everyone who's not completely paralyzed when he invented the boogie board.

The printing press had world-shaking consequences. And so can the boogie board. It doesn't just spread fun, it spreads joy and peace. How likely is it that a little kid who gets hooked on waves will become a Hitler and get hooked on hate and power when he grows up? Can you picture Stalin surfing? No tyrant was ever a surfer.

Look at those shiny little pieces of Heaven sticking out of that big, deep smile on the face of the eight year old who's just caught his first really good wave. Now tell me: when he grows up, is this kid going to find his jollies by planning how many millions of human bodies he can turn into corpses?

The three greatest Americans were all Georges. George Washington was the father of his country. George Freeth first brought the art of board surfing from Hawaii to California. He was the father of American surfing. And George Morey was the father of surfing democracy.

At the very least, the boogie board is up there with the ball and the spoon in technology's hall of fame.

A Defense of Bodyboarding: A Manifesto

There are at least 20 times more bodyboards than stand-up surfboards in America.

Nine out of ten people who own a bodyboard don't know how to use it.

There are hundreds of books that tell you how to use a stand-up surfboard.

Yet there are none that teach you how to use a bodyboard.

This situation must be remedied.

Almost everything you can do on a stand-up surfboard, you can do on a bodyboard. Notice, I didn't say "almost anything you can do on a *surf-board*, you can do on a bodyboard" because a body-board *is* a surfboard, even though stand-up surfers sometimes call them "sponges" and bodyboarders "spongers." Ignore them. Sticks and stones will break your bones but names will never hurt you.

They're just jealous that you can do with such ridiculous ease what they can do only by considerable practice and athleticism.

When you were a kid, you didn't start your self-transportation life by learning to drive a car. You first learned to ride a bike. Every human endeavor is like that: it makes sense to start the easy way.

But riding a bike is not a compromise. It's better than driving a car. It's simpler, cheaper, healthier, more environmentally sensitive, and more fun. It plunges you into nature and other people rather than isolating you. You actually talk to the people you pass. You slow down and smell the flowers. Ignorant or jealous drivers may call bicycles "training wheels," or "kiddie cars," but cyclists just ignore them and enjoy themselves.

The parallel with the bodyboard is obvious.

* * * * *

Here are seven reasons to choose to use a bodyboard.

1. I prefer a bodyboard to a stand-up board for the same reason I prefer an open convertible to a closed car, a glider to an airplane, and a bike to a car: to be closer to nature.

Body-surfing is closest of all, but bodyboarding is a close second in closeness. (And it's *much* harder to get long or fast rides body-surfing than bodyboarding.) On a bodyboard you get real "up close and personal," or real "down and dirty," with the sea. Your whole body is in it, not just your board. You're more like a fish. Bodyboarding is like riding a horse bareback; stand-up surfing is like riding a horse standing up in the stirrups.

2. It's egalitarian. Bodyboarders, or boogieboarders, are plunged into humanity as they are plunged into the sea. Not everybody can surf, but everybody can boogie. And millions do. Even me. I'm old. I'm clumsy. I can't dance or ice skate. But I can boogie. Ninety year olds can boogie. Two year olds can boogie.

3. When you bodyboard, since your whole body is in the water, your soul is too, since your soul is where your body is. (Unless you're having an out-of-body experience, and if you have an out-of-body experience in the ocean and your soul leaves your body, your soul will not go to the land. It will *become* the ocean.)

4. It's natural. Dolphins, ducks, seals, and fish don't stand up riding a wave.

5. It's easy. It's great for your self-esteem. It takes at the most a few hours to learn good body-boarding; it can take months or even years to learn good stand-up surfing. And as you're learning to be better, you're already riding nearly every wave. You feel like a success from day one.

6. It's safe. There's no hard board and no sharp fin. Your head won't get knocked unconscious by a little torpedo and your jugular vein won't get cut by a rudder.

7. Best of all, it lacks prestige. Board surfers are so jealous they call us names. They call us "spongers." This to me is a plus, not a minus. There's a whole bullshit surfing culture out there, but there's no such thing as bodyboard culture.

We could also add that if you're a man on a boogie board, you are the boogie man. So you don't have to be afraid of the boogie man any more.

Bodyboarding for Beginners: Seven Lessons

Lesson One: How to Wait

We don't begin by catching waves. We begin by waiting.

All good surfing begins with waiting.[5]

(1) The first waiting is waiting with your eyes, watching: watching the swells and the waves, first from the beach and then from the water. See how they look different from those two different perspectives. See where they are breaking. See what other surfers are doing with them.

---

5 All great art begins with waiting. A famous Taoist painter, told by the Emperor that he must paint bamboo for his Throne Room that would look so real to visitors that they would not know it was painted, and that he had to complete the job in 30 days or lose his head, spent 29 days and nights living in the fields of bamboo, then spent 23 of his last 24 hours simply holding brush and paints in his hand, and 59 of the last 60 minutes standing stock still before an empty wall. Then, in the last 60 seconds, there emerged from his brush the most miraculously lifelike bamboo ever painted.

(2) Another waiting is waiting with your ears, listening. (This is not essential to surfing itself, but it adds to its pleasure by expanding your sensory awareness; it helps you get acquainted with waves; and it teaches you to notice what you don't usually notice. All these are arts of living as well as surfing.) For a few minutes, pay attention only to the sounds, but pay full attention. Hear what you never heard before: how seagulls sound like something halfway between trumpets and kazoos, and how the happy voices of little kids blend together in a chorus like charismatics singing in tongues. And listen for the four sounds waves make.

Waves make four sounds because they die in four stages. The more you ride them, the more you learn to listen for these stages, as a hospice nurse learns to listen for the stages of dying.

First, the swell just before the wave breaks produces a sound that you can't hear with your ears at all but only with your bones. It's too deep for the ear. To the ear, it's silence; but it's the silence of the wave drawing its breath, ready for its suicide plunge.

Second, there is the sudden thunder of its break. When you hear this, you know why the

Greeks called it the voice of a god, Poseidon Earthshaker.

Third, there is the hiss of the foam as it slithers shoreward like a trapped snake.

Fourth, there is the burble of bubbles as the wave gently disappears into the sands. Here, at its oldest age, at the point of death, it sounds like a newborn baby gurgling happily.

(3) A third waiting is waiting with your skin: feeling. Here are five things to feel or taste while you are waiting for the wave:

(a) Feel the salty wind. Open your mouth wide and taste it.

(b) Feel the pulsing sunlight. Feel not just the heat on your face but even the brightness on your eyeballs.

(c) Feel the dancing sea sweeping you up in her arms, the rocking pressure of the passing swells.

(d) Twirl your tongue around your lips and savor the wild, salty taste of your own salted skin. Enlarge the area of your ecstasy by tasting the salt on all reachable flesh around your lips, extending your tongue like an anteater. Taste the hairy back of your hand. You are becoming an "old salt."

(e) Feel the swoosh of sand or the solidity of

clay beneath your bare feet. Send your soul down into the soles of your feet to feel this up-rush of divine grace.

Now reflect on the fact that through all these parts of the body you are feeling the whole world against your skin. These are five of *its* fingers.

These feelings are all very physical but also very holy. They are not necessarily sexual, but they are sensual. "Sensual" is not the opposite of "spiritual." You can feel the sea cleaning your spirit through your senses, through your skin and your lungs and your nose and your lips. For your soul is everywhere in your body, not tucked away in some dark little box of electrodes somewhere inside your brain!

You can do this even when there are no rideable waves at all. And when there are, you can ride them. You can't lose.

* * * * *

Surfing in New England teaches waiting.
Not all surfers live in Hawaii, California, or Australia. It just seems that way. Every California surfer I have ever talked to has shown pity or surprise at the fact that I am a New England surfer. The best way to defend and explain that masochistic

enterprise is to recount a conversation I had with a California surfer once (in California, in the waves). Let's call him "Duke."

When he found out where I lived, Duke's first question was: "What are you doing living in New England if you're a surfer?"

"What am I doing? For nine months I'm waiting for summer. Then, during the summer, for 80 days I'm waiting for surf on Lake Atlantic. Then, for 10 days, I'm surfing. That's what I'm doing in New England."

"You can surf here in California every day."

"I know. I like it better there."

"You're crazy. Or else you're not really a surfer. You don't really love to surf."

"Oh, but I do. That's why I like it there. I want to keep being in love with it. I don't think I'd be as much in love with it in California. I think I'd take it for granted. The romance would dry up."

"No way, man. That's just sour grapes. We got surfing *life* here. You're not into *life*, out there, man, you're just into *waiting* for life, or hoping for life. It's the Red Sox that do that to you."

"But I *am* into life. That's why I like New England. Surfing is more like life there: short and sweet. It's the short that makes it so sweet. Look, it's just like life and death: if you thought you were going to live for a thousand years, you'd be even more laid back and mellow and bored and spoiled than you are."

"Gee, thanks for the compliment."

"Don't you see my point?"

"Yeah, but it's not true. By your logic Hawaii would be even worse than California."

"Right."

"So you don't *like Endless Summer*?"

"The movie? I love it. But I'm glad I don't live in an endless summer."

"So you don't really like summer."

"Just the opposite. I love summer, but if I lived where it was summer all year, I'd never get that high in June when it comes again. Or that feeling of deep satisfaction that I get every April when I realize that I got through another New England winter. It's all about appreciation. Tell me, who appreciates summer more, Mediterraneans or Scandinavians?"

"I don't care. I'll take the Mediterranean."

I tried another approach. "Don't you put a high value on being creative?"

"Sure. What's that got to do with it?"

"We New Englanders have to be creative with

our surfing. We don't have much to work with. We're like the poor. We appreciate every penny."

"Oh."

"And what about wisdom? Don't you put a high value on wisdom?"

"What's that got to do with it?"

"Patience makes you wise. We wait years for a great wave, and we become deep and wise like the wave itself. You wait only a few seconds, and become airheads."

"Ooh, another compliment. Thanks. I don't believe a word you say, man. If you're a surfer, there's no way you can like Lake Atlantic better than Paradise Pacific. There's nothing worse than flat seas to a surfer."

"We have flat seas, but you have flat souls."

"Compliment number three. Thanks for the third time. Prove it, man. Why do we have flat souls?"

"Because there's no difference between one day and another in your paradise. To you, waves are like air."

"But when do you get to ride great waves? There aren't any really great waves in New England."

(Now I really started to tease him.) "Not true.

There *are* great waves in New England. I know. I was there. It was in 1976, I think. On a Friday afternoon there was one."

"What do you do all day while you wait for waves?"

"We think."

"You'll grow old waiting for a good wave there."

"No I won't. I only grow old on land. On the sea, I grow young."

I obviously didn't convince Duke. Frankly, I only half-convinced myself. (I lie a lot. I even lie about lying a lot.)

Lesson Two: How to Wipe Out

Surfing is a win-win-win situation, because there are only three possibilities for each wave: either you catch it, or you miss it, or you wipe out. Each way, you win.

Catching it is pure joy. You will remember your first wave all your life, like your first love. After you catch your first wave, you will be hopelessly "lost" forever, like Jack London on pages 16–17.

Missing the wave is frustrating but it doesn't hurt, and you can still live in hope. You are Romeo and you are serenading Juliet and she won't come elope with you yet, but she will sometime, in fact probably in just a few minutes! And even when you miss the wave, you are still in the biggest, healing-est, healthiest, most happifying thing on earth: the sea.

The third possibility is wiping out: a neglected pleasure.

Wipeouts are not to be feared. They can be far more fun than missing the wave entirely. A good wipeout is almost as good as a good ride. Catching a wave is like eloping with Juliet; missing the wave is like missing Juliet; and wiping out is like mud wrestling with Juliet.

The key to a good wipeout is just two things,

one physical and one mental: just (1) lie down and (2) enjoy it. There is an ecstasy under the scrapes and bruises and swallowed salt water, and the churning and pounding and sucking and somersaults in nature's biggest washing machine. The ecstasy is a kind of return to the womb of the Great Mother, knowing she will play with you as gently or as roughly as you let her. (Wipeouts don't just "happen." You invite them.) The fear is part of the delight. Your very helplessness is your greatest thrill. It's a little like sexual orgasm that way.

In fact, even uptight people who never let themselves go, especially into that state where they just can't stop laughing and shouting for pure joy like lunatics or little kids – even these people sometimes can do that in the sea. And those who fear the total loss of control that is death can sometimes learn from the sea the joy of total abandonment, and overcome the fear of death by tasting the joy in that abandonment – by wiping out on a wave, of all things.

But keep the ego on a leash, like a watchdog, so you don't let the monster smash your body into pieces in your mystic ecstasy. It's not a death wish. I was once body-surfing in the dangerously powerful swells that followed a hurricane (in the early Sixties, in Wildwood, New Jersey), and my logic almost killed me. For I had lost all fear because I knew the following syllogism was infallibly logical:

First premise: I have become the ocean.

Second premise: The one thing that cannot possibly drown in the ocean is the ocean.

Conclusion: I cannot possibly drown in the ocean.

Fortunately my ego barked in time.

* * * * *

What happens in a wipeout? Most wipeouts go "over the falls" into the giant's foamy mouth. The first thing that will happen is that you will be parted from your board, as you will be parted from your body at death.

If you use a leash, you will not lose your board, unless the wave is very strong ("really, really gnarly," if you live in Southern California). But you will probably get knocked in the gut or the head by it. On the other hand, if you don't use a leash, you will lose your board a few times. But you will almost always get it back. The sea is a gypsy: she freely steals and freely gives. Only once have I ever seen a bodyboard carried out to sea and not returned. Bottom line: if you fear pain more than poverty, don't use a leash.

Waves part you from your board as death parts you from your body. This is another way a wipeout is good rehearsal for death: you must let your board go, as you must let your body go. Don't try to grab at it. You have as much chance of keeping your board in a wipeout as you have of keeping your body in death. (The difference is that in death your body goes down and you (hopefully) go up, while in a wipeout you go down and your board goes up, into the sky like a kite.)

You will be swallowed by the wet whale, like Jonah. Don't fight the whale. Enjoy the trip into its mouth. Taste its salty saliva. Say, "Hello, whale." You are returning to the womb, so just roll yourself into a fetal ball, so your arms and legs don't get moving in opposite directions (*that* can be painful!). Then just let yourself sink down as far as you can. There is calmer water below the surface turbulence of the wave. You will usually find it.

Sometimes you won't. That's OK too. Just keep sinking into the white stuff. You are buoyant; you will come up again. Just try not to swallow too much water. (A little won't hurt you.)

How many socks have you lost in the wash? Now you will follow them and solve one of the great mysteries of human life: what happens to all those missing socks? They just seem to disappear out of the universe through a Black Hole. The socks are like time, like all the time our plethora of technological time-saving devices "save" for us: see page 4.

After one or two laundry cycles, you will emerge out of the washing machine. Unfor-tunately, sometimes you will emerge just in time to be crushed by a second wave. That's fine. Don't panic. Just remember to take a quick deep breath before you go down again. Now that you know what it's like, the second time is easier than the first – on your mind, at least. You came up the first time, and you'll come up the second time too. Whatever does not kill you makes you stronger.

If you come up with minor scrapes and cuts and bruises, stay in the water. There's nothing better than salt water for minor scrapes and cuts and bruises. The same Big Mama that slapped you will now kiss your boo-boos.

If you're surfing on a hard board, be sure you go down far enough to avoid being hit by your board. I do not recommend beginners using a leash on a hard board. I know a beginner who was hit in the neck by his longboard because the leash wouldn't let him let go of it in a wipeout. It put him in a body cast for six months. This is a big advantage of the bodyboard; it hits you only with a soft left jab.

And of course, if you're bodysurfing, there's no board at all to worry about.

If you're a beginner on a stand-up board, start with one of those specially designed longboards or shortboards for beginners that are soft and safe like bodyboards.

The very best way to avoid wipeouts is – to catch the wave!

Lesson Three: How to Find a Good Wave (and other miscellaneous advice)

1. First, find a good break. (A "break" is simply a place where waves break.) The ideal break for bodyboarding is a gradual, gently sloped bottom with waves breaking far enough out from shore (usually on a sandbar) to give you a good long ride in to the beach but close enough to shore so that you don't have to go out into water over your head if you're not a good swimmer.

Each break is different. Each beach is different. Each state is different. Each coast is different. For instance, the waves in the Pacific have much more speed and heaviness than the waves in the Atlantic.

2. To be rideable, the waves should be more than a foot high (unless you are a mouse). But don't try anything over five feet high at first. Work your way up gradually.

3. Look for an offshore wind (one that blows off the land toward the sea). An offshore wind holds up the face of the waves and gives them surfable form. An onshore wind (one that blows onto the land from the sea) blows off the tops of the waves and usually messes up their form.

4. Find a place where the waves are neither gently spilling horizontal "sissy waves" nor smashing, slamming vertical "sledgehammer waves."

There are two kinds of breaking waves. "Plunging" waves are waves that suddenly roll over into hollow tubes like barrel hoops. If they roll forward and don't move right or left they are called "close-out sets" (sets of waves) and are not good for surfing because you can't slide down their face nor can you catch them as they break without being "creamed." They just send you down, vertically, rather than shoreward, horizontally.

"Spilling" waves are the other kind. They spill over horizontally rather than falling vertically. They look like milk bubbles boiling over. When they are small and gentle; they lack the force to be rideable. So the ideal wave is either (a) a large, powerful spilling wave, or (b) a well-formed, sideways-moving plunging wave, or (c) a wave halfway between these two.

5. To find beaches with waves on any given day, use surf reports on the web or on the phone (most surf shops will give you daily surf reports), or even (in some places) in the newspaper, which usually reports at least the height of "seas" (swells).

6. Watch out for "rips" (rip currents) at all

times, but especially when the sea is most interestingly active. Rips are common enough to be the number one cause of drownings at sea. Watch for them *before* you go in the water.

You need to know (1) how to identify a rip and (2) how to swim out of one if you get caught in it. (1) Look for a stream of water moving out to sea, away from the shore, or sideways rather than shoreward (this is often the beginning of a rip). (2) If you get caught in a rip, do *not* to try to swim directly back to shore against that strong current that's carrying you out, because you'll just tire yourself out. It's stronger than you are. Instead, let it carry you and swim with it but at an angle to it, 90 degrees if you can, parallel to the shoreline, until it dumps you out of it. It always will, but sometimes not until you've let yourself get carried out a ways. If you are not a strong swimmer, don't take any chances: don't go in the ocean until you make sure there are no rips.

And if you can't swim at all, learn before you try in the ocean; it's not a big wading pool.

7. If you are right handed, hold your board as you would hold a woman dancing. Your left hand should grasp the "northwest corner" of the board, at the top (holding her upheld hand), while your right

hand should be almost halfway down the right hand side (on her waist). This maximizes control, and lets you turn the board in the wave. Once you are on the wave, you might want to move both hands forward to thrust the board down and forward more; this sometimes increases your speed. But if you push it down too much, you will "pearl" (topple over forward).

8. If you are at all imaginative, personalize your board by giving it a name and a distinctive mark. That helps it to become an extension of your body rather than a foreign object that you try to manipulate and control. It's all in your mind, of course, but your mind and your body always mutually reinforce each other.

9. By the way, don't pay less than $50 or more than $125 for your first bodyboard. The really expensive ones are for "high performance" beyond most beginners' capacities. The really cheap ones are for little kids and are too small, too spongy, and too thin. Be sure the bottom is hard and smooth, not soft, and that the rails (sides) are over 2 inches thick.

Lesson Four: Two Easy Ways to Catch Waves

Wave-catching is an art, and like every art you learn it only by doing it. It's more intuitive than rational. You just sense the right moment and catch the wave as it breaks. You catch the art of catching the wave in the same way as you catch the wave. Waves are like measles: you just catch them. Measles can't be taught, only caught. And once you catch one, you can catch them all. (There's no such thing as a single measle.)

Yet we can say some useful things about the art.

(1) The first way to catch a wave is the best and most basic way. Position yourself 5–10 feet farther out than the point where the wave will break. (Of course, you don't know exactly where the wave will break ahead of time, so you just have to watch the other waves and "guesstimate." You will get better at this the more you practice it.) Wait for a good-sized swell that is going to break into a wave at that exact "break point." Just as the swell arrives, a split second before the wave breaks, throw yourself and your board into it shoreward. Imagine you are throwing yourself onto a horse running past you, or a bus or a train. If you wear swim fins (they help a lot), swim into it as hard as you can.

Start a little earlier than you think you need to, because on your first few tries you will almost certainly be too late. Swells move faster than you think.

Kick those swim fins like crazy as you swim into the wave, and keep kicking as you take off on it. Don't be passive, be receptive.

You have to catch the curl of the wave, the white lip on top, just as it breaks. Therefore, you deliberately place yourself in the "impact zone" (unless the wave is a "sledgehammer" wave). This goes against your natural instincts, for the "impact zone" is the most dangerous spot. But you want to get hit with the wave's most powerful force, its first and strongest slap.

You don't just "place yourself" in the impact zone, of course; you swim or jump as fast as you can *into* it, from your position about 5–10 feet further out than the "break point," timing your arrival to coincide with the wave's breaking.

Do NOT put yourself into the impact zone of waves over six feet high ("overhead" sets), especially if they are vertically "plunging" rather than horizontally "spilling" waves, unless you are a masochist. Way #1, finding the impact zone and jumping into it, is for waves that are less than six feet high and that "spill," or break more gradually, with white foam starting at the top and then cascading down the face of the wave. You want to ride the foam, by getting just in front of it.

If you're in deep water when you catch the wave, and you have to swim into it rather than jumping off the bottom, you definitely want a good pair of stiff swim fins (*not* long, floppy diver's fins) to add to your speed and control as you swim into the wave. Swim fins help even if you're *not* in deep water as the wave breaks and you *are* able to push off shoreward from the bottom, jumping onto the wave rather than swimming into it. For even then, you *can* swim into it; and however you get into it, once you are on the wave, the swim fins will add to your speed and control. But if you don't like them, don't use them. They make you like a seal in the water (fast and graceful) but also like a seal on the land (slow and clumsy).

(2) The second way is the safer way. It almost seems like cheating, it's so easy. But if you are not a strong swimmer you should use this way for big, strong waves that break fairly far out from shore, whether they are plunging or spilling waves. Instead of catching them just as they break (which is dangerous for beginners with big waves), catch

them as soon *after* they break as it's safe, and ride the white foam to shore.

The closer you get to the point where the wave first breaks, the longer and faster your ride will be. Sometimes you can catch a big plunging wave on its first "bounce," which is usually about 10 or 15 feet from where it plunges (the impact zone). Even beginners can ride major waves this way, by riding the "foamie." If the wave is even bigger, too big to catch it on the first "bounce" safely, then try the "second bounce." A high plunging wave often has a second bounce, like a ground ball on a rough infield.

The third baseman, at the "hot corner," often has to decide instantly, by intuition, whether to field a hard-hit grounder on its first or second bounce. The first is faster but the second is safer. I call the wave's second bounce the "spit bounce." If you spit on a sidewalk, your spit sometimes bounces. An ant would be crushed by the first bounce, but not by the second. You are the ant, and the monster wave is a giant's spit.

The first time you find waves big enough to ride this way, you will probably be amazed at how much faster they push you than smaller waves do. Waves big enough to "bounce" have much greater power and speed. But watch out for the suck-back or "undertow": that will also have greater power and speed.

Way #2 is mainly for very powerful waves. Three things add to a wave's power: its height, its thickness (how much water is in it), and its speed. Way #2 means that you don't have to sacrifice stoke for safety. In fact, way #2, even though it's the safer way, can sometimes give you an even bigger stoke, simply because you're riding a bigger wave.

Lesson Five: Seven Kinds of Rides

The best thing to do while you wait for
perfect waves is to ride imperfect waves.
That's an underrated joy.

Most waves are far from perfect. Don't under-
estimate the imperfect. Everything but God is
imperfect in some way. Most rides are also imperfect, even on perfect waves. If you are a "soul-
surfer" (pages 34 ff.), then even an imperfect ride
on a perfect wave can give you a higher stoke than
a perfect ride on an imperfect wave. If you are a
"macho-surfer," it's the opposite.

Here is a road map of seven roads to Paradise:
seven kinds of rides.

1. **A miss:** the swell just goes over you and the
wave waves goodbye. You only ride the swell by
bobbing up and down. It's still nice – no lake or
pool can do it – but it's not a ride.

2. **A mugging:** the wave breaks too soon and
the foam shoves you around – maybe toward shore,
maybe not.

3. **A pony ride:** the wave breaks on you in foam
but you catch the middle of the foam instead of the

breaking tip, or lip. The foam then carries you only part of the way to shore, and not very fast.

4. **A roller coaster**: a catch that bumps you up and down as the turbulent whitewater carries you quickly to shore.

5. **A spank**: you catch the wave at exactly the point of maximum impact, and it spanks you on the seat of your pants (or the back of your bodyboard). You zoom out, riding in front of the whitewater. Your face is in the air, not in the foam, as it is in (3) and (4). You go all the way to the beach, as fast as the leading edge of the wave. This is the basic bodyboard ride, Perfect Ride #1.

6. **A water slide**: you slide *down the face* of the breaking wave, looking like a "real" surfer. This is Perfect Ride #2. See Lesson 6, coming up.

7. **A birth canal**: you do a free fall down the face of a plunging wave and you stay in the barrel of the wave for a few seconds of eternity. This is Perfect Ride #3, the Green Room, or the green cathedral. Welcome to Paradise! (See Lesson 7.)

Lesson 6: How to Ride Down the Wave Face

Only after mastering the two basic, beginners' ways in Lesson 4, and not before, are you ready for two more advanced ways of wave riding. Here you will learn to make your bodyboard do the same things that you see stand-up surfers make their boards do in surf videos and photos. One way is riding down the face of a breaking wave, at a slant, and the other is riding in the barrel of a hollow tube, or the "Green Room." (Lesson 7).

To ride down the face of a wave, you need a sizeable wave with a sizeable face. Three-foot waves are just too small. You also need waves of a certain shape: ones that are halfway between the mushy, foaming, gradually spilling kind (which *have* no face, only foam) and the vertically plunging "close-out" kind, which don't propel you right or left but just gobble you up where you are.

Here, instead of catching the breaking lip of the wave, as you did in the basic way #1, you catch its slanting *face* just before it breaks, or *as* it is breaking continuously right or left. Instead of riding the wave to the beach, you ride *down* the face, at an angle, following the way the wave is breaking, right or left.

When you first do this, you will feel four wonderful new things. First, you will feel the transfer of energy from you to the wave, as "I caught it" is transformed into "It caught me." This is smoother and less violent than being spanked by the breaking foam.

Second, you will get a much longer ride by following the wave horizontally as it continues to peel right or left. Though you are falling *down* the face, you don't reach the bottom because the wave continually rises up beneath you to present more face to ride.

Third, you will feel yourself falling down the wave's face vertically, not just being pushed to shore horizontally, and you will therefore feel much greater speed than when you ride the wave to the shore, because gravity is helping you accelerate. It will feel not just like *more* speed but a different *kind* of speed, a different category, a different quality of speed.

Fourth, despite the additional speed (or maybe because of it), you may feel everything suddenly stop and go silent at that point where you are at the top of the wave and about to slide down its face. It may feel as if God suddenly pushed the freeze-frame button. Sound takes time to travel, so sound will stop too. There is not enough time in that instant for any sound.

And then everything will suddenly begin again as you begin to fall down the face of the wave. You have just touched the edge of eternity and now you have come back into time.

A practical footnote: as you slide down the wave, the water will try to raise the nose of your board. Push down on the nose enough to keep the board level with the water (but not too much, or you'll "pearl"). Most beginners stall after takeoff because their board's nose is in the air. Don't let your board be a snob.

Lesson 7: How to Get in the Green Room

The last step in bodyboarding begins with the previous one, Lesson 6, and extends it. This is to ride along a large, hollow wave inside the tube, and then have the wave spit you out horizontally, like a giant snorting sideways from his nose.

The three qualifications for waves that you can ride this way are (1) that the form of the wave has to be more plunging than spilling for there to even *be* a hollow tube, (2) that it has to peel left or right rather than "close out," and (3) that it must be big enough for you to fit inside. Actually, you have an advantage over stand-up surfers here in that you can ride smaller tubes with bodyboards than with stand-up boards because you are plunked down on your board instead of standing up on it; your head will not touch the ceiling.

The "Green Room," or the "green cathedral," gives you another category-climb, another *kind* of stoke. You are in the eye of the hurricane, the still point of the turning world. This can be an intensely embodied out-of-body experience. You die and go to Heaven for a second.

Only after you master the two beginners' ways (Lesson 5) should you go on to the advanced way (Lesson 6, riding down the face), and only after you master that, should you knock on the door of the Green Room (Lesson 7). Don't try them in reverse order. The three stages of bodyboarding (Lessons 5, 6, and 7) are like the three stages of everything, the three stages of life: first you crawl, then you walk, then you run. First you get into your mother's womb, then you get into the world, then you get into Heaven.

Non-Conclusion

There is no conclusion to Paradise.